The Fascinating Journey of Jake Paul:

A History

By Howard N. Myer

The Fascinating Journey of Jake Paul

Copyright © 2023 by Howard N. Myer

All rights reserved. No part of this book may be reproduced or transmitted in any form or by any means, electronic or mechanical, including photocopying, recording, or by any information storage and retrieval system, without permission in writing from the publisher.

This book is protected by copyright. It may not, in whole or in part, be copied, photocopied, reproduced, translated, or reduced to any electronic medium or machine-readable form, in any form or by any means, without the prior written consent of the publisher.

The Fascinating Journey of Jake Paul

Table of Contents

Chapter One: Introduction

Chapter Two

Chapter Three

Chapter Four

Chapter Five

Chapter Six

Chapter Seven

Chapter Eight

Chapter Nine

    The Impact of Jake Paul's Endorsements and Professional Boxing Career

Chapter Ten

Chapter Eleven: Jake Paul's Awards and Accomplishments

Chapter Twelve: Conclusion

The Fascinating Journey of Jake Paul

Chapter One: Introduction

Jake Paul is one of the most popular entertainers and social media stars of the 2020s. He rose to fame in 2013, when he started posting comedic videos on the Vine platform. In 2017, Jake moved to Los Angeles and joined the cast of the Disney Channel series Bizaardvark, playing the role of Dirk.

Since then, Jake has become a household name and has millions of followers across all of his social media platforms. He has a successful YouTube channel with over 20 million subscribers and his videos have earned him over 1 billion views. He also has a music career, having released two albums and numerous singles.

In 2021, Jake started a production company, Team 10, which focuses on creating content for digital platforms. He also released his line of merchandise and apparel and has a podcast, Impulsive, that has over 3 million subscribers.

In addition to his entertainment career, Jake is also an entrepreneur. He has invested in several companies, including a real estate company, a lifestyle brand, a cryptocurrency, and a venture capital fund.

Jake Paul is one of the most influential figures of his generation and his career is still on the rise. His future looks bright and it will be interesting to see what he does next.

Chapter Two

Jake Paul is one of the most successful social media personalities of the 21st century. He has gained worldwide fame for his comedic and often outrageous YouTube videos, his social media presence, and his music career.

He is an American actor, YouTube star, and professional boxer. He first gained fame on the now-defunct app Vine and has since become a household name due to his YouTube channel and other social media platforms. He is also well-known for his philanthropy and professional boxing career.

Born in Cleveland, Ohio, in 1997, Jake Paul was the youngest of four children. His parents, Greg and Pamela Paul were both real estate agents. Growing up, Jake was a creative and outgoing child. He was particularly passionate about sports, especially football, and wrestling. Jake often played pranks on his siblings, and his outgoing personality made him popular in school.

In his teenage years, Jake's interest in comedy and entertainment grew. He began uploading comedic skits to the popular video-sharing website Vine. His videos gained a large following online, and in 2013, he was offered a role on the Disney Channel show Bizaardvark

In 2016, Jake Paul released his first single, entitled "It's Everyday Bro". The song was an instant hit, and it quickly gained over 100 million views on YouTube. His videos continued to be incredibly popular and Jake Paul's fame only grew.

Jake Paul's success on YouTube led to various endorsement deals and sponsorships. He was featured in advertisements for companies such as Pepsi and American Eagle. He also signed a deal with Disney to become an Ambassador for the company's social media presence.

Jake Paul also ventured into the music industry. He released his first EP in 2017, which was titled "It's Everyday Bro". The EP featured popular songs such as "It's Everyday Bro" and "Ohio Fried Chicken".

In 2018, Jake Paul released his first full-length album, "Disaster Boy". The album featured a mix of hip-hop, pop, and rock music, and it was well-received by critics. The album charted in the top ten of the Billboard 200 chart, and it was certified Gold in the United States by the Recording Industry Association of America.

Jake Paul has become an icon in the social media world and beyond. He has over 20 million subscribers on YouTube, and he has over 11 million followers on Instagram. He is also a successful entrepreneur, having launched his merchandise line and co-founded a talent management company.

Overall, Jake Paul's success on social media and in the music industry is remarkable. From his humble beginnings making skits for Vine, he has risen to become one of the most famous personalities of the 21st century. His ambitious nature and creative spirit have allowed him to create a successful career and achieve worldwide fame.

Chapter Three

Paul's music career began in 2015 when he started releasing singles on iTunes and Spotify. He had already gained a large following on the app Vine, where he was known for his comedic videos. His early singles, such as "Kissin You" and "My Life Is Lit", were generally well-received, and helped him build a loyal fanbase.

Paul continued to release new music throughout 2016. He released his first full-length album, It's Everyday Bro, in May of that year. The album, which was named after his breakthrough single, was met with mixed reviews, but still managed to reach #3 on the Billboard 200, and spawned several hit singles, including "Litmas", "Ohio Fried Chicken", and "Frick Da Police".

In 2017, Paul released his second full-length album, Team 10. The album, which was produced by Grammy-nominated producer

MikeWillMadeIt, was met with more positive reviews than his previous work. It charted at #7 on the Billboard 200 and featured the hit single "Jerika", which was certified platinum by the Recording Industry Association of America (RIAA). The album also spawned other successful singles, such as "21st Century Vampire" and "It's Everyday Bro".

Paul's music has been described as a mix of rap, pop, and EDM. His songs often have humorous and lighthearted lyrics and have been compared to the work of artists such as Lil Yachty and Lil Uzi Vert. He has also collaborated with other artists, such as rapper Gucci Mane and singer Noah Cyrus.

In addition to his music career, Paul has also had success as an actor and YouTube star. He has appeared in films such as Airplane Mode and The Thinning and was a contestant on the Fox reality show The Masked Singer. He also has a popular

YouTube channel, which has over 19 million subscribers and over 4 billion views. On his channel, he often posts vlogs and sketches, as well as music videos for his songs.

Overall, Jake Paul has experienced great success in the music industry. He has released several hit singles and albums, and his songs have been streamed millions of times. He has also established himself as a successful actor and YouTube star.

Chapter Four

Jake Paul is an American internet personality, actor, and rapper. He is best known for his YouTube channel and as one of the early members of the Vine phenomenon. Paul gained fame through his Vine career and later transitioned into acting, appearing in films such as 'Dance Camp' and 'Mono'. He also starred in the YouTube Red series 'Team 10' and 'The Thinning'.

Paul began his acting career in 2015 with a guest appearance on the Disney Channel show 'Bizaardvark'. He then starred as Dirk in the 2016 YouTube Red movie 'Dance Camp', and in the same year, he appeared in the movie 'Mono'. Following this, he joined the cast of the Disney Channel series 'Bizaardvark' for a recurring role in 2017.

In the same year, he appeared in the YouTube Red series 'Team 10', in which he and his friends created content for the channel.

In 2018, Paul starred in the YouTube Red series 'The Thinning', a sci-fi thriller set in a world where population control is enforced through a school exam. He also starred in the 2018 movie 'Airplane Mode', in which he plays a vlogger who is stuck on a plane with no Wi-Fi. He then starred in the 2019 movie 'The Space Between Us', a romantic drama in which he plays the love interest of a girl living on Mars.

In 2020, Paul starred in the Netflix movie 'The Devil All the Time', playing a small-town pastor with a dark past. He also appeared in the YouTube series 'Foursome', playing the role of a high school student. He is set to star in the upcoming Netflix movie 'Love and Monsters', in which he plays an obnoxious monster hunter.

Despite his success in acting, Paul has been the subject of much criticism. He has been accused of being insensitive and homophobic in his videos, and he has been involved in several controversies, such as a feud with fellow YouTuber KSI. He has also been accused of exploiting his young fans for money.

Regardless of the criticism, Paul has continued to be active in the entertainment industry. He has released several rap songs and music videos, and he has been active in the charity sector, donating money to some causes. He also starred in the movie 'Law & Order: Special Victims Unit' in 2020.

Paul achieved success in the entertainment industry at a young age, and he is proof that hard work and dedication can lead to success. He is an inspiration to many young people who want to pursue a career in the entertainment industry.

Chapter Five

In 2020, Paul announced that he would pursue a career in professional boxing. He made his professional debut in January 2021 when he defeated fellow YouTuber AnEsonGib in a six-round fight. Since then, Paul has gone on to win three more professional fights.

Paul's boxing career has been a source of much controversy. His opponents have often been accused of not being legitimate boxers, and many critics have questioned his motivations for entering the sport. Despite this, Paul has continued to pursue his boxing career and has become one of the most popular boxers in the world.

In this article, we will take a look at Jake Paul's professional boxing career. We will explore his rise in the sport, his opponents, and his plans.

The Fascinating Journey of Jake Paul

Jake Paul started his boxing career in 2020 when he announced his intention to pursue a professional boxing career. He signed a multi-fight deal with Showtime Sports and his first bout was held on January 30, 2021. His opponent was fellow YouTuber AnEsonGib. The fight was scheduled for six rounds, and Paul won by a technical knockout in the second round. The fight was widely viewed on pay-per-view and was highly successful.

After his successful debut, Paul went on to fight two more opponents. On April 17, 2021, he faced former MMA fighter Ben Askren and won by technical knockout in the first round. On August 28, 2021, Paul faced ex-NBA player Nate Robinson and won by knockout in the second round.

Paul has become one of the most popular boxers in the world. His fights have been widely viewed on pay-per-view and have become some of the most widely watched boxing events in history. Paul has also been highly successful in terms of sponsorship and endorsement deals. He has inked deals with brands such as Adidas, Reebok, and Monster Energy.

Paul's opponents have often been criticized for not being legitimate boxers. Despite this, Paul has continued to pursue his boxing career and has become one of the most popular boxers in the world.

Paul has also been involved in controversies outside of the ring. He has been accused of bad sportsmanship and taunting his opponents. In 2021, he was involved in a physical altercation with rapper Dillon Danis.

Despite the controversies, Paul has continued to build his boxing career. He has expressed a desire to fight some of the biggest names in the sport such as Floyd Mayweather and Conor McGregor. Paul has also expressed interest in fighting YouTuber KSI.

Paul has also expressed a desire to become an ambassador for the sport. He has said that he wants to use his platform to reach out to young people and inspire them to pursue a career in boxing.

Chapter Six

Paul's social media presence has been growing ever since he started his YouTube channel in 2013. He now has over 20 million subscribers, and his videos have been viewed over 4 billion times. On top of that, he has a large presence on other social media platforms such as Instagram, Twitter, and Facebook. He is constantly engaging with his fans, posting content, and interacting with them.

Paul's social media presence isn't just about promoting himself. He uses it to promote his other projects and businesses, such as his clothing line and TV show. He also uses it to promote his charity work, such as his Team Ten Foundation, which helps disadvantaged youth. In addition, he uses it to engage with his fans in a meaningful way, such as by hosting Q&As and responding to their comments. By doing this, he can build relationships with his fans and create a strong connection with them.

Paul's professional boxing career is relatively new, but he has made a huge impact in the sport. He made his debut in 2020, and he has already won two of his three fights. He's an aggressive fighter with a lot of power, and he has been praised by the boxing community for his technique and skill. He has also gained a lot of attention for his involvement in the sport, as he often speaks out about the politics and issues in the boxing world.

Paul's social media presence and professional boxing career go hand in hand. He uses social media to promote his fights, giving his fans a chance to see him in action. He also uses it to engage with his fans, giving them a chance to get to know him better and build a connection with him. By doing this, he can create a larger fan base and a better understanding of himself and his career.

Overall, Jake Paul has been able to leverage his social media presence to create a successful career in boxing. His content and engagement with his fans have allowed him to gain a large following and a strong connection with them. This has in turn led to his success in the sport, and he is now one of the most popular boxers in the world.

Chapter Seven

Jake Paul's philanthropy is one of the most notable aspects of his career. He has been involved in various charitable organizations, such as the Make-A-Wish Foundation, which grants wishes to children with life-threatening illnesses.

He has also been involved in fundraising for St. Jude Children's Research Hospital, and the Make-A-Wish Foundation. Jake Paul has also donated to the Red Cross, in response to the devastating effects of Hurricane Harvey in 2017.

In addition to his charitable endeavors, Jake Paul is also known for his professional boxing career. He first made his debut in the boxing ring on November 9, 2018, when he faced fellow YouTuber Deji Olatunji. He went on to fight fellow YouTuber KSI in November 2019 in a highly publicized match that was broadcast on pay-per-view. While

The Fascinating Journey of Jake Paul

KSI ultimately won the fight, Jake Paul has since gone on to fight former NBA player Nate Robinson in a highly anticipated match in November 2020.

While Jake Paul's professional boxing career has been met with mixed reviews, he has managed to earn considerable success within the sport. He is currently ranked in the Top 10 in the WBA's super middleweight division and is the #2-ranked light heavyweight in the world. He has also been featured in multiple boxing magazines and was even the subject of a GQ magazine profile.

Apart from his career in professional boxing, Jake Paul is also known for his philanthropic activities. He has been involved in a variety of charitable organizations, such as the Make-A-Wish Foundation, St. Jude Children's Research Hospital, and the Red Cross. He has also been involved in various fundraising efforts, such as the #TsunamiRelief campaign, which raised more than $500,000 for those affected by the 2011 tsunami in Japan.

In addition to his philanthropic activities, Jake Paul has also been involved in various educational initiatives. He has spoken at Harvard Business School and has been involved in various mentorship initiatives. He has also been involved in the development of the "Career Accelerator" program, which is designed to help young people develop the skills and resources necessary to start their businesses.

Jake Paul is an influential figure in the world of philanthropy and professional boxing. His charitable contributions, mentorship initiatives, and educational efforts have helped to make a positive impact on the world. He is an example of how one person can make a difference in the lives of others, and his career serves as an inspiration to many.

Chapter Eight

Jake Paul is a polarizing figure in the world of entertainment. The YouTube star has been involved in some controversies over the years, ranging from his career choices to his personal life. In addition, Paul has recently entered the world of professional boxing, despite being a novice in the sport. In this article, we will examine some of the controversies that have surrounded Jake Paul, and his fledgling professional boxing career.

Jake Paul first rose to fame in 2013, when he began posting videos on the now-defunct app Vine. Paul quickly amassed millions of followers and became known for his outlandish pranks and stunts. He eventually moved to YouTube, where he has continued to post comedic and music videos that have earned him millions of subscribers.

In addition, Paul has been criticized for his lifestyle choices. In 2017, he was criticized for throwing a large party at his home, which resulted in the police being called and citations being issued. Paul was also criticized for his alleged involvement in several fights, including a street fight in 2019.

More recently, Paul has been criticized for his foray into professional boxing. Paul made his professional boxing debut in January 2020, when he faced fellow YouTuber AnEsonGib in a match that was streamed on pay-per-view. Paul won the match but was criticized for his lack of boxing skills and for being a novice in the sport.

Since then, Paul has faced off against former NBA player Nate Robinson in a match that was streamed on the streaming service Triller. Paul won the fight but was again criticized for his lack of skill and for using his celebrity status to gain access to the professional boxing world.

Despite the criticisms, Paul's boxing career has been successful so far. He has signed a multi-million dollar deal with Showtime, and he is set to face off against former MMA fighter Ben Askren later this year.

Chapter Nine

Jake Paul has managed to secure a number of lucrative endorsement deals with a variety of different companies. In 2018, Paul signed an endorsement deal with the clothing line, 'Champion'. Under the terms of the deal, Paul was given several free items from the clothing line and the opportunity to promote Champion on his social media accounts.

In 2019, Paul signed a deal with the energy drink company, 'Bang'. This deal saw Paul promote Bang on his social media accounts and make several promotional appearances for the company. The deal also included some free energy drinks for Paul to give away to his fans.

In 2020, Paul signed a deal with the shoe company, 'Reebok'. This deal saw Paul appear in a number of promotional videos for the company and promote Reebok on his social media accounts. He was also given many free items from the Reebok range to give away to his fans.

In 2021, Paul signed a deal with the fast-food restaurant, 'Chipotle'. This deal saw Paul promote Chipotle on his social media accounts and make some promotional appearances for the company. He was also given some free Chipotle items to give away to his fans.

Jake Paul has also made several deals with other companies, including the gaming company, 'EA Sports', the streaming service, 'Twitch', and the streaming platform, 'YouTube'. All of these deals have helped Paul to further his career by providing him with a source of additional income and allowing him to reach a larger audience.

The Impact of Jake Paul's Endorsements and Professional Boxing Career

Jake Paul's endorsements and professional boxing career have had a significant impact on his overall career. His endorsement deals have provided him with a source of additional income, enabling him to further his career and reach a larger audience. His professional boxing career has also helped him to gain more exposure, with his fights being broadcasted to millions of viewers around the world.

The success of Paul's professional boxing career has also helped to legitimize him as a professional athlete, with many fans now viewing him as a legitimate boxer rather than just a YouTube star. This has helped to raise his profile and expand his fanbase, allowing him to pursue other opportunities, such as acting and hosting.

Overall, Jake Paul's endorsements and professional boxing career have had a major impact on his overall career. His endorsement deals have provided him with additional income and a larger platform to reach a wider audience, while his boxing career has helped him to legitimize himself as a professional athlete. As a result, Paul has been able to further his career and gain more exposure, setting the stage for future success.

Chapter Ten

Jake Paul is an American YouTuber, boxer, and entrepreneur. He has amassed a large following on YouTube and Instagram, and his success continues to grow. Paul has leveraged his social media fame to create multiple business ventures, launch a professional boxing career, and become a successful entrepreneur.

Paul's business ventures began in 2015 when he created Team 10, a YouTube-based talent collective. Team 10 was designed to help up-and-coming social media influencers grow their brands and develop their businesses.

Team 10 members were given the opportunity to collaborate on projects, receive training and advice from Paul, and gain access to exclusive events. This venture quickly grew in popularity, and Paul eventually launched a clothing line, Team 10 Merch.

In 2018, Paul founded the clothing company, Unbroken. The company is a lifestyle apparel brand that seeks to inspire others to "break the mold and stand out from the crowd." Paul is deeply involved in all aspects of the business, and he has been seen modeling the clothing on his Instagram page. Unbroken has become a popular streetwear brand and has been worn by numerous celebrities, including Justin Bieber and Hailey Baldwin.

In 2019, Paul launched the online marketing agency, Maverick Agency. The agency is designed to help brands and influencers build their digital presence and grow their businesses. Maverick Agency works with brands to help them create effective marketing campaigns, increase their online visibility, and develop their social media presence. The agency has since grown in size, and Paul has been featured in various publications as a digital marketing expert.

In addition to his business ventures, Paul has also dabbled in professional boxing. In 2020, he made his professional boxing debut against fellow YouTuber, AnEsonGib. The fight was a success, and Paul won by TKO in the first round. Paul has since gone on to fight several professional boxers, including former NBA player Nate Robinson. Paul has been praised for his skill in the ring, and he has become a fan favorite for his entertaining style of boxing.

Paul's business ventures, social media presence, and professional boxing career have helped him become a successful entrepreneur. His entrepreneurial spirit, drive, and vision have enabled him to create multiple successful businesses, launch a professional boxing career, and amass a large following on YouTube and Instagram. As his success continues to grow, there is no telling what other business ventures Paul will pursue in the future.

Chapter Eleven: Jake Paul's Awards and Accomplishments

Paul has earned several awards and accolades throughout his career. In 2017, he was named Social Star of the Year at the 10th Annual Shorty Awards. He was also named Most Popular Viner in the 2016 Teen Choice Awards. In addition, Paul was nominated for the 2017 Kids' Choice Award for Favorite Social Media Star. He is also the recipient of the 2017 Teen Choice Award for Choice YouTuber.

Paul's professional boxing career has been controversial and has gained a lot of attention in the media. Paul made his professional debut in January 2020 and won his first match against British YouTuber AnEsonGib. He then went on to win his second fight against fellow YouTuber Deji Olatunji. Paul then competed in the celebrity match against former NBA star Nate Robinson and won the match by knockout in the 2nd round.

Paul's next bout was against former MMA fighter Ben Askren, which ended in a controversial stoppage in the first round. Paul continued his professional boxing career by competing in an exhibition match against former 4-division world champion Floyd Mayweather Jr. Despite going the distance, Paul lost the match by unanimous decision. In his most recent bout, Paul faced off against former UFC fighter Tyron Woodley, winning the fight by technical knockout in the second round.

Paul has also made several appearances in the media. He has been featured in several magazines, including GQ, Maxim, and Forbes. In addition, Paul has made several television appearances, including on The Tonight Show with Jimmy Fallon, Jimmy

Kimmel Live!, and The Ellen DeGeneres Show.

Paul has also been involved in various charitable initiatives. He has raised money for several causes, including for the victims of the 2017 Hurricane Harvey in Houston, Texas. He has also raised money for the Special Olympics and the Boys & Girls Club of America.

Overall, Jake Paul is an accomplished professional boxer, YouTuber, and social media influencer. He has earned several awards and accolades for his career, including the Social Star of the Year award at the 10th Annual Shorty Awards and the 2017 Teen Choice Award for Choice YouTuber. In addition, Paul has made several appearances in the media and has been involved in various charitable initiatives. He continues to entertain and inspire his millions of fans around the world.

Chapter Twelve: Conclusion

Jake Paul has created a unique and controversial presence in the social media landscape. His rise to fame began in 2013 when he first started making YouTube videos, and his career has seen a meteoric rise since then. He has become a major figure in the world of entertainment, and his work has been featured on television, in movies, and even in video games.

His success has come with its share of controversy, as he has been accused of bullying, inappropriate language, and other issues. Despite this, Jake Paul has become a household name, with millions of followers and fans around the world. His influence has been felt in the music, film, and television industries and his success will continue to be felt in the years to come.

Printed in Great Britain
by Amazon